The Jumbo Jokes

and Riddles Book

for Kids (Part 2)

Over 700 Hilarious Jokes, Riddles and

Brain Teasers Fun for The Whole Family

DL Digital Entertainment
MADE TO ENTERTAIN

DL Digital Entertainment

3

TABLE OF CONTENTS

CHAPTER 1: INTRODUCTION

We would like to personally thank you for taking the time to purchase our book *The Jumbo Jokes and Riddles Book for Kids Part 2*. We've spent countless hours putting together only the best, laugh out loud jokes for you, the kids and the family to enjoy! You can expect to find in the first half of this book over 700 jokes put into categories such as knock, knock, silly, food, doctor-doctor, animal, spooky and school. The second half of this book will be focused on Riddles and Brain Teasers These jokes and riddles are guaranteed to make you laugh hard, test your brain and have all kinds of fun with the kids, friends and family!

The Jumbo Jokes and Riddles Book Part 2 is very versatile thanks for it also being available in audio format on audible.com! Use it on your own before bed, with friends at a get together, with family at the dinner table or camping with relatives; the possibilities with *The Jumbo Jokes and Riddles Book* are endless. Be creative and utilize it to its full potential!

CHAPTER 2: WHY JOKES AND RIDDLES?

This ultimate assortment of jokes for kids, family and friends will not only make you laugh but do so in a fun and interactive way. Jokes have been around since the dawn of time and have many other benefits such as:

-Confidence Boosting: With so many kids and people in general struggling with self-confidence in our day and age, listening and interacting with these jokes and riddles in a safe environment with family and friends gives them the opportunity to comfortably say answers and repeat hilarious jokes and riddles, giving them the ability to not be afraid to express themselves.

-Relieve Stress: Jokes help in relieving your anger, depression, tension and stress and make you feel light and irritation free. It also improves the mood by reducing

anxiety and fear. Laughter increases heart rate and blood pressure, both of which cools down your stress response.

-Improved Bonding: The Jumbo Jokes and Riddles Book is one of the best ways for friends and family to spend time with each other and build positive, healthy relationships through laughter and participation when listening to the jokes and trying to answer the questioning ones.

-Personal Health: Jokes make us laugh and impacts the body in a very positive way. When you start to laugh, it not only lightens your body but also induces many physical changes in it as well. Not only that, but funny jokes boost up the human immune system by increasing infection fighting antibodies.

-Reduce Boredom: Having a book such as The Jumbo Jokes and Riddles Book gives you the ability to have fun and entertainment on demand.

-Develop Humor: Jokes and riddles sharpen your sensibilities and tune our capabilities. It improves your personality by bringing out your lighter side. Humor also allows people to express their feelings without any hesitation.

Now, that's enough talking. Are you ready to get started with *The Jumbo Jokes and Riddles Book.* Awesome! Let's Begin.

CHAPTER 3: KNOCK, KNOCK JOKES

A smile is the light in your window that tells others that there is a caring, sharing person inside.

Denis Waitley

1. Knock, knock.

Who's there?

Canoe.

Canoe who?

Canoe help me with my homework?

2. Knock, knock

Who's there?

Merry.

Merry who?

Merry Christmas!

3. Knock, knock.

Who's there?

Orange.

Orange who?

Orange you going to let me in?

4. Knock, knock.

Who's there?

Anee.

Anee,who?

Anee one you like!

5. Knock, knock

Who's there?

Iva.

Iva who?

I've a sore hand from knocking!

6. Knock, knock.

Who's there?

Dozen.

Dozen who?

Dozen anybody want to let me in?

7.   Knock, knock.

Who's there?

Needle.

Needle who?

Needle little money for the movies.

8.   Knock, knock.

Who's there?

Henrietta.

Henrietta who?

Henrietta worm that was in his apple.

9.   Knock, knock.

Who's there?

Avenue.

Avenue who?

Avenue knocked on this door before?

10. Knock, knock.

Who's there?

Harry.

Harry who?

Harry up, it's cold out here!

11. Knock, knock.

Who's there?

A herd.

A herd who?

A herd you were home, so I came over!

12. Knock, knock.

Who's there?

Adore.

Adore who?

Adore is between us. Open up!

13. Knock, knock.

Who's there?

Otto.

Otto who?

Otto know. I've got amnesia.

14. Knock, knock.

Who's there?

King Tut.

King Tut who?

King Tut-key fried chicken!

15. Knock, knock.

Who's there?

Lettuce.

Lettuce who?

Lettuce in it's cold out here.

16. Knock, knock.

Who's there?

Noah.

Noah who?

Noah good place we can get something to eat?

17. Knock knock.

Who's there?

Mustache.

Mustache who?

I mustache you a question, but I'll shave it for later.

18. Knock knock.

Who's there?

Tank.

Tank who?

You're welcome.

19. Knock knock.

Who's there?

I smell mop.

I smell mop who?

Ew.

20. Knock knock.

Who's there?

I eat mop.

I eat mop who?

That's revolting.

21. Knock knock.

Who's there?

Ya.

Ya who?

Yahoo! I'm just as psyched to see *you*!

22. Knock knock.

Who's there?

Voodoo.

Voodoo who?

Voodoo you think you are, asking me so many questions?

23. Knock knock.

Who's there?

Spell.

Spell who?

Okay, okay: W. H. O.

24. Knock knock.

Who's there?

Candice.

Candice who?

Candice door open, or what?

25. Knock knock.

Who's there?

Boo.

Boo who?

No need to cry, it's only a joke.

26. Knock knock.

Who's there?

Stopwatch.

Stopwatch who?

Stopwatch you're doing and pay attention!

27. Knock knock.

Who's there?

To.

To who?

It's to *whom.*

28. Knock knock.

Who's There?

Dewey.

Dewey who?

Dewey have to use a condom *every* time?

29. `Knock knock.

Who's there?

Honey bee.

Honey bee who?

Honey bee a dear and open up, would you?

30. Knock knock.

Who's there?

Lettuce.

Lettuce who?

Lettuce in, it's cold out here!

31. Knock knock.

Who's there?

Mikey.

Mikey who?

Mikey doesn't work so help me out, would you?

32. Knock knock.

Who's there?

Dwayne.

Dwayne who?

Dwayne the bathtub already. I'm drowning!

33. Knock knock.

Who's there?

Razor.

Razor who?

Razor hands, this is a stick up!

34. Knock knock.

Who's there?

Olive.

Olive who?

Olive *you*. Do you love me too?

35. Knock knock.

Who's there?

Alec.

Alec who?

Alec-tricity. Ain't that a shocker?

36. Knock knock.

Who's there?

Howl.

Howl who?

Howl you know unless you open the door?

37. Knock knock.

Who's there?

Iran.

Iran who?

Iran all the way here. Let me in already!

38. Knock knock.

Who's there?

Says.

Says who?

Says me, that's who.

39. Knock knock.

Who's there?

Snow.

Snow who?

Snow use askin' when you can just open.

40. Knock knock.

Who's there?

Some.

Some who?

Someday you'll recognize me, hopefully.

41. Knock knock.

Who's there?

Stupid.

Stupid who?

Stupid *you*, that's who.

42. Knock knock.

Who's there?

Needle.

Needle who?

Needle little help gettin' through.

43. Knock knock.

Who's there?

Thermos.

Thermos who?

Thermos be a better way to get through to you.

44. Knock Knock

Who's there?

Water.

Water who?

Water you doing? Just open the door!

45. Knock knock.

Who's there?

Amos.

Amos who?

A mosquito.

46. Knock knock.

Who's there?

Dozen.

Dozen who?

Dozen anyone wanna let me in?

47. Knock knock.

Who's there?

Nanna.

Nanna who?

Nanna your business, that's who.

48. Knock knock.

Who's there?

Euripides.

Euripides who?

Euripides jeans, you pay for 'em, okay?

49. Knock knock.

Who's there?

Annie.

Annie who?

Annie way you can let me in soon?

50. Knock knock.

Who's there?

Canoe.

Canoe who?

Canoe come out or what?

51. Knock, knock.

Who's there?

Robin.

Robin who?

Robin the piggy bank again.

52. Knock, knock.

Who's there?

Dwayne.

Dwayne who?

Dwayne the bathtub, It's overflowing!

53. Knock, knock.

Who's There?

Imma.

Imma Who?

Imma gettin' old open the door!

54. Knock, knock.

Who's there?

Banana.

Banana who?

55. Knock, knock.

Who's there?

Orange.

Orange who?

ORANGE YOU GLAD I DIDN'T SAY BANANA!

56. Knock, knock.

Who's there?

Boo.

Boo who?

Gosh, don't cry it's just a knock knock joke.

57. Knock, knock.

Who's There?

Impatient cow.

Impatient cow wh-?

Mooooo!

58. Knock, knock

Who's there?

A little old lady.

A little old lady who?

I didn't know you could yodel.

59. Knock, knock

Who's there?

Sadie.

Sadie who?

Sadie magic word and watch me disappear!

60. Knock, knock,

Who's there?

Olive.

Olive who?

Olive you!

Will you remember me in 2 minutes?

Yes.

61. Knock, knock.

Who's there?

Hey, you didn't remember me!

62. Knock, knock.

Who's there?

Justin.

Justin who?

Justin time for dinner.

63. Knock, knock.

Who's there?

Kirtch.

Kirtch who?

God bless you!

Will you remember me in a minute?

Yes.

Will you remember me in a week?

Yes.

Will you remember me in a year?

Yes.

64. Knock, knock.

Who's there?

Cash.

Cash who?

No thanks, I'll have some peanuts.

65. Knock, knock.

Who's there?

Luke.

Luke who?

Luke through the peep hole and find out.

66. Knock, knock.

Who's there?

Ivor.

Ivor who?

Ivor you let me in or I`ll climb through the window.

67. Knock, knock.

Who's there?

Claire.

Claire who?

Claire the way, I'm coming through!

68. Knock, knock.

Who's there?

Arfur.

Arfur who?

Arfur got!

69. Knock, knock.

Who's there?

Abby.

Abby who?

Abby birthday to you!

70. Knock, knock.

Who's there?

Ya.

Ya who?

Wow. You sure are excited to see me!

71. Knock, knock.

Who's there?

Cows go

Cows go who?

Cows don't go who, they go moo!

72. Knock, knock.

Who's there?

Etch.

Etch who?

Bless you!

73. Knock, knock.

Who's there?

Roach.

Roach who?

Roach you a letter, did you get it?

74. Knock, knock.

Who's there?

Aida.

Aida who?

Aida sandwich for lunch today.

75. Knock, knock.

Who's there?

Iona.

Iona who?

Iona new car!

76. Knock, knock.

Who's there?

Scold.

Scold who?

Scold enough out here to go ice skating.

77. Knock, knock.

Who's there?

Police.

Police who?

Police hurry up, it's chilly outside!

78. Knock, knock

Who's there?

Justin.

Justin who?

Just in the neighborhood, thought I would drop by.

79. Knock, knock

Who's there?

Ben.

Ben who?

Ben knocking For 10 minutes.

80. Knock, knock.

Who's there?

Two knee.

Two knee who?

Two-knee fish!

81. Knock, knock.

Who's there?

Hoo.

Hoo who?

Are you a owl?

82. Knock, knock.

Who's there?

I am.

I am who?

You mean you don't know who you are?

CHAPTER 4: SILLY JOKES

Smile in the mirror. Do that every morning and you'll start to see a big difference in your life.

Yoko Ono

1.   What goes up and down but does not move?

Answer: Stairs

2.   Where should a 500 pound alien go?

A: On a diet

3.   What did one toilet say to the other?

A: You look a bit flushed.

4.   Why did the picture go to jail?

A: Because it was framed.

5.   What did one wall say to the other wall?

A: I'll meet you at the corner.

6.   What did the paper say to the pencil?

A: Write on!

7.   What do you call a boy named Lee that no one talks to?

A: Lonely

8.   What gets wetter the more it dries?

A: A towel.

9.   Why do bicycles fall over?

A: Because they are two-tired!

10. Why do dragons sleep during the day?

A: So they can fight knights!

11. What did Cinderella say when her photos did not show up?

A: Someday my prints will come!

12. Why was the broom late?

A: It over swept!

13. What part of the car is the laziest?

A: The wheels, because they are always tired!

14. What did the stamp say to the envelope?

A: Stick with me and we will go places!

15. What is blue and goes ding dong?

A: An Avon lady at the North Pole!

16. Were you long in the hospital?

A: No, I was the same size I am now!

17. Why couldn't the pirate play cards?

A: Because he was sitting on the deck!

18. What did the laundryman say to the impatient customer?

A: Keep your shirt on!

19. What's the difference between a TV and a newspaper?

A: Ever tried swatting a fly with a TV?

20. What did one elevator say to the other elevator?

A: I think I'm coming down with something!

21. Why was the belt arrested?

A: Because it held up some pants!

22. Why was everyone so tired on April 1st?

A: They had just finished a March of 31 days.

23. Which hand is it better to write with?

A: Neither, it's best to write with a pen!

24. Why can't your nose be 12 inches long?

A: Because then it would be a foot!

25. What makes the calendar seem so popular?

A: Because it has a lot of dates!

26. What is green and has yellow wheels?

A: Grass.....I lied about the wheels!

27. What is it that even the most careful person overlooks?

A: Her nose!

28. Did you hear about the robbery last night?

A: Two clothes pins held up a pair of pants!

29. Why do you go to bed every night?

A: Because the bed won't come to you!

30. Why did Billy go out with a prune?

A: Because he couldn't find a date!

31. Why do eskimos do their laundry in Tide?

A: Because it's too cold out-tide!

32. How do you cure a headache?

A: Put your head through a window and the pane will just disappear!

33. What has four wheels and flies?

A: A garbage truck!

34. What kind of car does Mickey Mouse's wife drive?

A: A minnie van!

35. Why don't traffic lights ever go swimming?

A: Because they take too long to change!

36. Why did the man run around his bed?

A: To catch up on his sleep!

37. Why did the robber take a bath before he stole from the bank?

A: He wanted to make a clean get away!

38. Why do birds fly to warmer climates in the winter?

A: It's much easier than walking!

39. What creature is smarter than a talking parrot?

A: A spelling bee.

40. How does the ocean say hello?

A: It waves.

41. What do you call a fake noodle?

A: An im-pasta.

42. Why can't you trust atoms?

A: They make up everything.

43. What did one plate whisper to the other plate?

A: Dinner is on me.

44. Why aren't dogs good dancers?

A: They have two left feet?

45. What do you call an old snowman?

A: Water.

46. Why was the picture sent to jail?

A: It was framed.

47. How do you get a tissue to dance?

A: You put a boogie in it.

48. Why did the banana go to the hospital?

A: He was peeling really bad.

49. Which superhero hits the most home runs?

A: Batman.

It Has Wheels and Flies

50. Why is a baseball stadium always cold?

A: Because it's full of fans!

51. What are the strongest days of the week?

A: Saturday and Sunday. All the others are weekdays.

CHAPTER 5: FOOD JOKES

Your smile will give you a positive countenance that will make people feel comfortable around you.

Les Brown

1.   Why did the can crusher quit his job?

A: Because it was soda pressing.

2.   Why do hamburgers go to the gym

A: To get better buns!

3.   How much room is needed for fungi to grow?

A. As mushroom as possible

4. What happened after an explosion at a French cheese factory?

A: All that was left was de brie.

5. Why did the butcher work extra hours at the shop?

A: To make ends meat

6. Who's a dessert's favorite actor?

A: Robert Brownie, Jr.

7. When do you go at red and stop at green?

A: When you are eating a watermelon

8. What do you call cheese that is sad?

A: Blue cheese

9. Did you hear about the carrot detective?

A: He got to the root of every case.

10. What's the difference between a shamrock and a bread knife that gets used a lot?

A. The shamrock is a four-leaf clover, and the knife is a four-loaf cleaver.

11. What did the hot dog say when his friend passed him in the race?

A. Wow, I relish the fact that you've mustard the strength to ketchup to me.

12. Which thrill ride does a wine glass love to go on the most?

A. A coaster!

13. How do you keep intruders out of a castle made of cheese?

A. Moatzarella.

14. What do you call a grilled cheese sandwich that gets right up in your face?

A. Too close for comfort food.

15. Which type of vegetable tries to be cool, but is only partly successful at it?

A. The radish.

16. What do you call a round, green vegetable that breaks out of prison?

A. An escapea.

17. Why does yogurt love going to museums?

A. Because it's cultured.

18. What do you call a fake noodle?

A. An impasta.

19. Why did the dieter go to the paint store?

A: He wanted to get thinner.

20. Why do watermelons have fancy weddings?

A: Because they cantaloupe.

21. What does a grape say when it gets stepped on?

A: Nothing, it just l

22. What is black; white; green and bumpy?

A: A pickle wearing a tuxedo.

23. What do you call cheese that isn't yours?

A: Nacho cheese!

24. What kind of coffee was served on the Titanic?

A: Sanka!

25. What's the best thing to put into a pie?

A: Your teeth!

26. Waiter, this food tastes kind of funny?

A: Then why aren't you laughing!

27. Why did the fisherman put peanut butter into the sea?

A: To go with the jellyfish!

28. What did the baby corn say to its mom?

A: Where is popcorn?

29. What do you call candy that was stolen?

A: Hot chocolate!

30. What kind of nuts always seems to have a cold?

A: Cashews!

31. What is green and brown and crawls through the grass?

A: A Girl Scout who has lost her cookie.

32. What is white, has a horn, and gives milk?

A: A dairy truck!

33. What candy do you eat on the playground?

A: Recess pieces.

34. Why don't you starve in a desert?

A: Because of all the 'sand which is' there.

35. How do you make a walnut laugh?

A: Crack it up!

36. In which school do you learn to make ice cream?

A: Sunday School.

37. What are twins favorite fruit?

A: Pears!

38. If a crocodile makes shoes, what does a banana make?

A: Slippers!

39. How do you make a milk shake?

A: Give it a good scare!

40. What do you call a peanut in a spacesuit?

A: An astronut!

41. What kind of keys do kids like to carry?

A: Cookies!

42. Why don't they serve chocolate in prison?

A: Because it makes you break out!

43. What cheese is made backwards?

A: Edam.

CHAPTER 6: DOCTOR, DOCTOR!

Always wear a smile because you never know who is watching.

Gracie Gold

1. Doctor doctor, I've swallowed my pocket money

• Take this and we'll see if there's any change in the morning

2. Doctor doctor, what happened to that man who fell into the circular saw and had the whole left side of his body cut away?

• He's all right now.

3. Doctor doctor, I'm at death's door!

• don't worry, we'll soon pull you through

4. Doctor doctor, my spouse is so ill, is there no hope?

• it depends what you are hoping for

5. Doctor doctor, Help me now! I'm getting shorter and shorter!

- just wait there and be a little patient

6. Doctor doctor, I feel like a pair of wigwams

- the problem is, you've become too tense

7. Doctor, doctor I'm addicted to brake fluid

- Nonsense man, you can stop anytime

8. Doctor doctor, I couldn't drink my medicine after my bath like you told me

- why not?

well after I've drunk my bath I haven't got room for the medicine

9. Doctor doctor, every time I drink a cup of hot chocolate I get a stabbing pain in the eye

- Try taking the spoon out first

10. Doctor doctor, they've dropped me from the cricket team - they call me butterfingers

• don't worry, what you have is not catching

11. Doctor doctor, I'm really worried about my breathing

• We'll soon put a stop to that

12. Doctor, doctor, I've only got 59 seconds to live

• just wait a minute will you . . .

13. Doctor doctor, I've heard that exercise kills germs; is it true?

• Probably, but how do you get the germs to exercise?

14. Doctor, doctor I've become invisible

• I'm afraid I can't see you now

15. Doctor, doctor my nose runs and my feet smell

• I fear you might have been built upside down

16. Doctor, doctor I've broken my arm in two places

• hmm, I'd advise you not to go back to either of those places then

17. Doctor, doctor I keep thinking I'm a dog

• Sit on the couch and we will talk about it.

But I'm not allowed up on the couch!

18. Doctor doctor I've a strawberry stuck in my ear!

• Don't worry, I've some cream for that!

19. Doctor doctor I feel like a pony!

• don't worry, you're just a little hoarse!

20. Doctor doctor you said i'd be dead in ten - ten what? years? months?

• 10, 9, 8, 7, 6...

21. Doctor doctor I've become a kleptomaniac

• have you taken anything for it?

so far a TV, three sofas and a necklace

22. Doctor doctor an alternative medicine quack told us to put a LOT of goose fat all over grandad's back

• if you do that, he'll go downhill fast

23. Doctor doctor I've swallowed a fish bone.

• are you choking?

No, I really did!

24. Doctor, Doctor I'm scared of Father Christmas

• you're suffering from Claus-trophobia

25. Doctor, Doctor will this ointment clear up my spots?

• I never make rash promises...

26. Doctor doctor I keep seeing spots before my eyes

• have you seen a doctor already?

no, just spots

27. Doctor doctor every time I stand up quickly, I see Mickey Mouse, Donald Duck and Goofy

• how long have you been getting these disney spells?

28. Doctor doctor I can't help it, I just keep thinking I'm a moth

• you need a psychiatrist not a doctor

I know, but I was walking past and I saw your light was on.

29. Doctor, Doctor - I've got amnesia

• Just go home and try to forget about it...

30. Doctor, Doctor - they are saying in the waiting room that you've become a vampire...

• Necks please...

31. Doctor, Doctor - I keep singing "Green green grass of home" - I think I have Tom Jones syndrome

• It's not unusual...

32. Doctor, Doctor - Aaa, Eee, I, oooh! You...

• I think you may have irrtitable vowel syndrome..

33. Doctor doctor I can't help thinking I'm a goat

• how long have you felt like this?

Since I was a kid..

34. Doctor, I get a pain in my eye when I drink coffee.

Have you tried taking the spoon out of the cup?

35. Doctor, Doctor - I keep thinking I'm a caterpillar...

• Don't worry, you'll soon change...

36. Doctor I feel like biscuits

What, do you mean square ones?

Yes!

The ones you put butter on?

Yes!

Oh, you're crackers!!

37. Doctor, Doctor - I keep comparing things with something else.

• Don't worry, it's only analogy

38. Doctor, doctor, I think I need glasses.

You certainly do madam. This is a fish and chip shop!

39. Doctor, I've been thinking I may be a moth for some time now.

Really? So what made you call in to see me today?

Oh, I saw the light at the window...

40. Doctor, will this ointment clear up all my spots?

Well, I don't like to make rash promises.....

41. Doctor, doctor. I keep painting myself gold!

Mmm sounds like a gilt complex!

42. Doctor, Doctor, my baby's swallowed a bullet.

Well, don't point him at anyone until I get there!

43. Doctor: "You need new glasses"

Patient: "How do you know? I haven't told you what's wrong yet!"

Doctor: " I could tell as soon as you walked in through the window!"

44. Doctor, doctor, some days I feel like a marquee, and others I feel like a wigwam.

Yes, I can see you are two tents

(too tense)

45. Doctor doctor, I've swallowed my pocket money.

Take this and we'll see if there's any change in the morning

46. Doctor, doctor, I feel like a spoon.

Mmm, just sit there and don't stir!

47. "Doctor, doctor, will I be able to play the violin after the operation?"
"Yes, of course..."
"Great! I never could before!"

CHAPTER 7: ANIMAL JOKES

Let us always meet each other with smile, for the smile is the beginning of love.

Mother Teresa

1. What do you call a sleeping bull?

A: A bull-dozer.

2. How do you fit more pigs on your farm?

A: Build a sty-scraper!

3. What did the farmer call the cow that had no milk?

A: An udder failure.

4.   Why do gorillas have big nostrils?

A: Because they have big fingers!

5.   What do you get from a pampered cow?

A: Spoiled milk.

6.   Why are teddy bears never hungry?

A: They are always stuffed!

7.   Where do polar bears vote?

A: The North Poll

8.   What did the judge say when the skunk walked in the court room?

A: Odor in the court!

9.   Why are fish so smart?

A: Because they live in schools.

10. What do you call a cow that won't give milk?

A: A milk dud!

11. When is a well dressed lion like a weed?

A: When he's a dandelion (dandy lion)

12. How does a lion greet the other animals in the field?

A: Pleased to eat you.

13. What happened when the lion ate the comedian?

A: He felt funny!

14. What fish only swims at night?

A: A starfish!

15. Why is a fish easy to weigh?

A: Because it has its own scales!

16. What do you get when a chicken lays an egg on top of a barn?

A: An eggroll!

17. Why didn't the chicken cross the road?

A: Because there was a KFC on the other side!

18. Why did the chicken cross the road?

A: To show everyone he wasn't chicken!

19. Why did the lion spit out the clown?

A: Because he tasted funny!

20. Why did the turkey cross the road?

A: To prove he wasn't chicken!

21. What animals are on legal documents?

A: Seals!

22. What do you get when you cross a snake and a pie?

A: A pie-thon!

23. What time is it when ten elephants are chasing you?

A: Ten after one!

24. What wears glass slippers and weighs over 4,000 pounds?

A: Cinderellephant

25. What was the elephant's favorite sport?

A: Squash

26. How do you keep an elephant from charging?

A: You take away its credit cards!

27. What's the best thing to do if an elephant sneezes?

A: Get out of its way!

28. What do you do with a blue elephant?

A: You try and cheer her up

29. What is 'out of bounds'?

A: An exhausted kangaroo!

30. What did the buffalo say to his son when he went away on a trip?

A: Bison!

31. Why didn't the boy believe the tiger?

A: He thought it was a lion!

32. How do bees get to school?

A: By school buzz!

33. What do you call a bear with no ears?

A: B!

34. What animal has more lives than a cat?

A: Frogs, they croak every night!

35. What is a cat's favorite color?

A: Purrr-ple

36. What kind of kitten works for the Red Cross?

A: A first-aid Kit.

37. What's worse than raining cats and dogs?

A: Hailing' taxi cabs!

38. Why are cats good at video games?

A: Because they have nine lives!

39. Why can't a leopard hide?

A: Because he's always spotted!

40. What song does a cat like best?

A: Three Blind Mice.

41. What game did the cat like to play with the mouse?

A: Catch!

42. Why did the cat go to medical school?

A: To become a first aid kit

43. Who was the first cat to fly in an airplane?

A: Kitty-hawk

44. Have you ever seen a catfish?

A: No. How did he hold the rod and reel?

45. What state has a lot of cats and dogs?

A: Petsylvania

46. What time is it when an elephant sits on the fence?

A: Time to fix the fence!

47. Why did the elephant sit on the marshmallow?

A: So he wouldn't fall into the hot chocolate.

48. What would you do if an elephant sat in front of you at a movie?

A: Miss most of the film.

49. Why are elephants so wrinkled?

A: Did you ever try to iron one?

50. What do you do when you see an elephant with a basketball?

A: Get out of its way!

51. What is gray and blue and very big?

A: An elephant holding its breath!

52. There were 10 cats in a boat and one jumped out. How many were left?
    a. None, because they were copycats!

53. How did Noah see the animals in the Ark at night?
    a. With flood lighting.

54. What happened when 500 hares got loose on Main Street?
    a.   The police had to comb the area.

55. What do you give a dog with a fever?
    a.   Mustard, its the best thing for a hot dog!

56. How do spiders communicate?
    a.   Through the World Wide Web.

57. Why do cows have hooves instead of feet?
    a.   Because they lactose.

58. A man walks into a zoo, the only animal was a bat.
    a.   It was a batzu

59. What do you call shaving a crazy sheep?
    a.   Shear madness.

60. What do you call 2 octopuses that look exactly the same?
    a.   Itenticle.

61. Where did the cat go when it lost its tail?
    a.   To the retail store!

62. Where do you find a dog with no legs?
    a.   Where you left it.

63. Why is a bee's hair always sticky?
    a.   Because it uses a honey comb!

64. What animal has more lives than a cat?
    a.   Frogs, they croak every night!

65. What is a cat's favorite breakfast?
    a.   Mice krispies

66. Who makes dinosaur clothes?
    a.   A dino-sewer.

67. What do you call a dinosaur that never gives up?
    a.   A try and try and try-ceratops!

68. What pine has the longest needles?
    a.   A porcupine.

69. What do you do if your cat swallows your pencil?
    a.   Use a pen.

70. Why does a giraffe have such a long neck?
    a. Because his feet stink!

71. Why don't bears wear shoes?
    a. What's the use? They'd still have bear feet!

72. What do fish take to stay healthy?
    a. Vitamin sea.

73. How do you keep a skunk from smelling?
    a. Plug its nose.

74. What did the Cinderella fish wear to the ball?
    a. Glass flippers.

75. What do you get when you cross a roll of wool and a kangaroo?
    a. A woolen jumper!

76. Why are giraffes so slow to apologize?
    a. It takes them a long time to swallow their pride.

77. What is black and white and red all over?
    a. A skunk with a rash.

78. What was the first animal in space?
    a. The cow that jumped over the moon.

79. What do you call an exploding monkey?
    a. A baboom.

80. What do you call a cow in a tornado?
    a. A milkshake.

81. Which day do fish hate?
    a. Fryday.

82. How does a dog stop a video?
    a. He presses the paws button.

83. 40. What do you call a cow that eats your grass?
    a. A lawn moo-er.

84. What goes tick-tock, bow-wow, tick-tock, bow-wow?
    a. A watch dog.

85. What do you call a thieving alligator?
    a. A crookodile

86. Where did the sheep go on vacation?
    a. The baaaahamas

87. What do you do if your dog chews a dictionary?
    a. Take the words out of his mouth!

88. How do you count cows?
    a. With a cowculator.

89. Why couldn't the leopard play hide and seek?
    a. Because he was always spotted.

90. What did the elephant say to the man?
    a. "How do you breathe through something so small?"

91. Can a kangaroo jump higher than the Empire State Building?
    a. Of course. The Empire State Building can't jump.

92. What did the duck say when he bought lipstick?
    a. Put it on my bill.

93. What happens to a frog's car when it breaks down?
    a. It gets toad away.

94. Why are cats bad storytellers?
    a. Because they only have one tale.

95. What do you call a deer with no eyes?
    a. No-eye-deer.

96. For sale: Dead Canary.
    a. Not going cheep.

97. What's the cheapest kind of meat you can buy?
    A. Deer balls. They're under a buck.

98. Why did the lamb run over the cliff?
    a. He didn't see the ewe turn.

99. What do bees do if they want to use public transport?

a.   Wait at a buzz stop!

100.   What bird can be heard at mealtimes?
a.   A swallow.

101.   What kind of ant is even bigger than an elephant?
a.   A gi-ant

CHAPTER 8: SPOOKY JOKES

Share your smile with the world. It's a symbol of friendship and peace.

Christie Brinkley

1. On which day are ghosts most scary?

A. Fright-day!

2. What do witches put in their hair?

A. Scare spray!

3. What do spooks with poor eyesight wear?

A. Spook-tacles!

4. What day do ghosts do their howling?

A. On Moan-day!

5. Did you hear about the monster who ate his own house?

A. He was homesick.

6. What do you call a hairy monster in a river?

A. A weir-wolf!

7. Did you hear about the untidy cemetery?

A. You wouldn't want to be caught dead in there!

8. Why did the ghost go to the sales?

A. Because they were bargain haunters!

9. Why didn't the skeleton jump off the roof?

A. He didn't have the guts.

10. What do ghosts turn on in summer?

A. The scare-conditioner!

11. Why do ghosts hate rain?

A. It dampens their spirits.

12. What do you call a witch that lives at the beach?

A. A sand witch!

13. How do you make a witch scratch?

A. Take away the 'w'!

14. What is a spook's favourite ride?

A. A roller-ghoster!

15. What is a ghost's favourite dessert?

A. Boo-berries and I Scream!

16. Why do they have a fence around the graveyard?

A. Because everyone is dying to get in!

17. What did the wizard say to the twin witches?

A. Which witch is which?

18. What does a ghost do when he gets in the car?

A. Puts his sheet belt on!

19. Why did Dr Jekyll cross the road?

A. To get to the other Hyde!

20. Why do vampires always seem sick?

A. They're always coffin.

21. What's scarier than a monster?

A. A momster.

22. What do ghosts like do drink the most?

A. Ghoul-aid.

23. How does a witch style her hair?

A. With scare-spray.

24. Why did the werewolf go to the dressing room when she saw the full moon?

A. She needed to change.

25. Why did Ichabod Crane stop on the road?

A. The street sign said "Stop ahead."

26. What did Frankenstein say when he woke up from a nap?

A. "I've just had a shocking dream."

27. Why were Dracula's pancakes so terrible?

A. He got turned into the bat-ter.

28. What did the vampire say when she saw her reflection?

A. Time to get a new mirror!

29. What does Bigfoot say when he ask for candy?

A. Trick-or-feet

30. How many abominable snow monsters does it take to screw in a lightbulb?

A. Only one, but you have to believe in it first.

31. What kind of monster likes to dance?

A. The boogeyman.

32. Where do werewolves store their junk?

A. A were-house.

33. Where do ghosts like to go swimming?

Lake Erie.

34. What was the ghost's favorite band?

A. The Grateful Dead.

35. Why don't mummies have time for fun?

A. They are too wrapped up in their work.

36. Where does Dracula keep his money?

A. In a blood bank.

37. Why can't Dracula play baseball?

A. He lost his bat.

38. What does a ghost keep in his stable?

A. Nightmares.

39. What did the werewolf eat after his teeth cleaning?

The dentist.

40. What did the skeleton buy at the grocery store?

A. Spare ribs.

41. Why was the ghost crying?

A. He wanted his mummy.

42. Where does the zombie live?

A. On a dead end street.

43. What is a ghost's least favorite candy?

A. Life Savers.

44. What is a vampire's favorite dog?

A. A bloodhound.

CHAPTER 9: SCHOOL JOKES

I can't change my personality. I'll always smile, but I'll be more focused.

Katarina Johnson-Thompson

1. Why did the student throw his watch out of the school window?

A: He wanted to see time fly.

2. Why do they never serve beer at a math party?

A: Because you can't drink and derive...

3. What's another name for Santa's elves?

A: Subordinate Clauses.

4.   What's a teacher's favorite nation?

A: Expla-nation.

5.   Why didn't the skeleton go to the school dance?

A: He didn't have anybody to take. (any BODY)

6.   Why didn't the quarter roll down the hill with the nickel?

A: Because it had more cents.

7.   What is a chalkboard's favorite drink?

A: hot chalk-olate!

8.   What's the longest word in the dictionary?

A: Rubber-band -- because it stretches.

9.   If H2O is the formula for water, what is the formula for ice?

A: H2O cubed

10. Why don't farts graduate from high school?

A: Because they always end up getting expelled!

11. Why did the scientist go to the tanning salon?

A: Because he was a paleontologist.

12. Why wasn't the geometry teacher at school?

A: Because she sprained her angle!!

13. Name a bus you can never enter?

A: A syllabus

14. What did the mathematician's parrot say?

A: A poly "no meal"

15. How do the fish get to school?

A. By octobus!

16. What does a gorilla learns in school?

A. His Ape B C's.

17. What does a snake learn in school?

A. Hiss tory.

18. Why is 2+2=5 like your left foot?

It's not right.

19. Teacher: Can anyone tell me how many seconds there are in a year?

A. Student: 12! January 2nd, February 2nd, March 2nd...

20. Teacher: Johnny, which month has 28 days?

A. Student: Every month!

21. What did the glue say to the teacher?

A. "I'm stuck on you."

22. What do get when you cross one principal with another principal?

A. I wouldn't do it, principals don't like to be crossed!

23. What do you do if a teacher rolls her eyes at you?

A. Pick them up and roll them back to her!

24. Why are school cafeteria workers cruel?

A. Because they batter fish, beat eggs, and whip cream.

25. What flies around the kindergarten room at night?

A. The alpha-BAT.

26. What did the ghost teacher say to his class?

A. "Look at the board and I'll go through it again!"

27. Why is it dangerous to do math in the jungle?

A. Because when you add four and four you get ate

28. Why did 6 hate 7?

A. 7 8 9.

29. What did the math book say to the other math book?

A. "I've got problems."

30. Why didn't the class clown use hair oil the day before the big test?

A. Because he didn't want anything to slip his mind.

31. Why do teachers give you homework?

A. Just to annoy you.

32. What's the difference between a train and a teacher?

A. The teacher says, "Spit your gum out" and the train says, "Choo-........choo!"

33. Why is arithmetic hard work?

A. All those numbers you have to carry.

34. What did the student say after the teacher said, "Order students, order?"

A. "Can I have fries and a burger?"

35. Why did the new boy steal a chair from the classroom?

A. Because the teacher told him to take a seat.

36. When is a blue school book not a blue school book?

A. When it is read!

37. Where do New York City kids learn their multiplication tables?

A. Times Square.

38. What's the best place to grow flowers in school?

A. In kindergarden.

39. Why was the voice teacher so good at baseball?

A. Because she had the perfect pitch.

40. What's the worst thing that can happen to a geography teacher?

A. Getting lost.

41. Why did the teacher wear sunglasses?

A. Because his students were so bright!

42. Where do monsters study?

A. In ghoul school.

43. Teacher: Name two days of the week that start with "t".

A. Pupil: Today and Tomorrow.

44. What school supply is always tired?

A. A knapsack!

45. Teacher: I see you missed the first day of school.

A. Kid: Yes, but I didn't miss it much.

46. Teacher: Could you please pay a little attention?

A. Student: I'm paying as little attention as I can.

47. Teacher: James, where is your homework?

A. James: I ate it.

Teacher: Why?

James: You said it was a piece of cake!

48. Teacher: Why is your homework in your father's handwriting?

A. Pupil: I used his pen!

49. Teacher: You've got your shoes on the wrong feet.

A. Pupil: But these are the only feet I've got!

50. Today my teacher yelled at me for something I didn't do.

What was that?

A. My homework!

51. What is white when its dirty and black when its clean?

A. A blackboard!

52. When do astronauts eat?

A: At launch time!

53. What did the pencil sharpener say to the pencil?

A: Stop going in circles and get to the point!

54. How does the barber cut the moon's hair?

A: E-clipse it!

55. What happened when the wheel was invented?

A: It caused a revolution!

56. What is the world's tallest building?

A: The library because it has the most stories.

57. What vegetables to librarians like?

A: Quiet peas.

58. Why did the clock in the cafeteria run slow?

A: It always went back four seconds.

59. What did you learn in school today?

A: Not enough, I have to go back tomorrow!

60. What holds the sun up in the sky?

A: Sunbeams!

61. What did the ground say to the earthquake?

A: You crack me up!

62. Why did the music teacher need a ladder?

A: To reach the high notes.

63. What's the worst thing you're likely to find in the school cafeteria?

A: The Food!

64. What kind of plates do they use on Venus?

A: Flying saucers!

65. Why did nose not want to go to school?

A: He was tired of getting picked on!

66. What do you give to a sick lemon?

A.: Lemon aid

67. What's a tornado's favorite game to play?
    A: Twister

68. What do you get when you throw a lot of books in the ocean?
    A: A title wave

69. Why couldn't the bicycle stand up?
    A: Because it was two-tired

70. Why did the man take his clock to the vet?
    A: Because it had ticks

71. Which is faster – heat or cold?
    A: Heat, because you can catch a cold

72. What do you call a boomerang that doesn't come back?

A: A stick

73. Why did the chicken go to jail?
    A: Because he was using fowl language

74. What has two legs but can't walk?
    A: A pair of pants

75. What did the buffalo say at drop off?

A. Bison.

76. Why isn't there a clock in the library?

A. Because it tocks too much.

CHAPTER 10: PUNNY PUNS

"To succeed in life, you need three things: a wishbone, a backbone, and a funny bone."

Reba McEntire

1. What do you call an alligator in a vest?

A. An investigator.

2. This boy said he was going to hit me with the neck of a guitar.

I said, "Is that a fret?"

3. How many tickles does it take to make an octopus laugh?

A. Ten tickles.

4. Whiteboards are remarkable.
5. My leaf blower doesn't work.
   It sucks.

6. Insect puns bug me.
7. Would a cardboard belt be a waist of paper?
8. Never give your uncle an anteater.
9. I'm very good friends with 25 letters of the alphabet.

I don't know why.

10. I woke up this morning and forgot which side the sun rises from.

Then it dawned on me.

11. Learning how to collect trash wasn't that hard, I just picked it up as I went along.
12. A golf ball is a golf ball no matter how you putt it.
13. If you need help building an ark, I Noah guy.
14. My dog can do magic tricks.

It's a labracadabrador.

15. Never marry a tennis player.

Love means nothing to them.

16. I tried to catch some fog.

I mist.

17. I knew a couple who met in a revolving door.

I think they're still going round together.

18. Did you know taller people sleep longer in bed?
19. I heard a funny joke about a boomerang earlier.

I'm sure it'll come back to me eventually.

20. I asked the lion in my wardrobe what he was doing there, he said it was "Narnia Business".
21. Pencils could be made with erasers at both ends, but what would be the point?
22. I was struggling to figure out how lightning works then it struck me.
23. Sue broke her finger today, but on the other hand she was completely fine.
24. I've just been on a once-in-a-lifetime holiday.

I'll tell you what, never again.

25. I often say to myself, "I can't believe that cloning machine worked!"
26. Some people say I'm addicted to somersaults but that's just how I roll.

27. What do you call Dracula with hayfever? The pollen Count.
28. Never lie to an x-ray technician. They can see right through you.
29. My friend made a joke about a TV controller. It wasn't remotely funny.
30. I have a speed bump phobia but I'm slowly getting over it.
31. I'm working on a device that will read minds. I'd love to hear your thoughts.
32. I saw an advert that read: "Television for sale, $1, volume stuck on full." I thought to myself, I can't turn that down.

33. I thought about becoming a witch, so I tried it for a spell.
34. Those new corduroy pillows are making headlines.
35. When it comes to cosmetic surgery, a lot of people turn their noses up.
36. I went to a restaurant last night and had the Wookie steak. It was a little Chewy.
37. Broken puppets for sale. No strings attached.
38. Don't drink with ghosts, they can't handle their boos.
39. I asked my mom to make me a pair of pants. She was happy to, or at least sew it seems.
40. I applied for a job at the local restaurant. I'm still waiting.
41. I was going to look for my missing watch, but I could never find the time.
42. I've been learning braille. I'm sure I'll master it once I get a feel for it.
43. If a judge loves the sound of his own voice, expect a long sentence.

44. I just walked past a shop that was giving out dead batteries free of charge.
45. When it came to getting even with my local bus company, I pulled out all the stops.
46. The best way to communicate with fish is to drop them a line.
47. I used to be addicted to soap, but I'm clean now.
48. It was an emotional wedding. Even the cake was in tiers.
49. Once you've seen one shopping center you've seen a mall.
50. The person who invented the door knock won the No-bell prize.
51. Jokes about German sausage are the wurst.
52. Singing in the shower is all fun and games until you get shampoo in your mouth. Then it becomes a soap opera.
53. The other day someone left a piece of plasticine in my house. I didn't know what to make of it.
54. The other day a clown held the door open for me. I thought it was a nice jester.
55. I'd tell you my construction joke but I'm still working on it.
56. There was a recent study that tried to pinpoint the effect that alcohol had on walking. The result was staggering.
57. My Grandma is having trouble with her new stair lift. It's driving her up the wall.
58. To the guy who invented Zero: Thanks for nothing!
59. Have you ever tried to eat a clock? It's very time consuming.
60. What jumps from cake to cake and smells of almonds? Tarzipan.

61. There was a big paddle sale at the boat store. It was quite an oar deal.
62. I tried to finish the left-overs but... foiled again...
63. I really wanted a camouflage shirt, but I couldn't find one.
64. I couldn't work out how to fasten my seatbelt. Then it clicked.
65. Did you hear about those new reversible jackets? I'm excited to see how they turn out.
66. I'm glad I know sign language, it's pretty handy.
67. My friend's bakery burned down last night. Now his business is toast.
68. A man just assaulted me with milk, cream and butter. How dairy.
69. When the cannibal showed up late for lunch, the others gave him the cold shoulder.
70. A small boy swallowed some coins and was taken to hospital. When his grandmother telephoned to ask how he was, the nurse said "No change yet".
71. How does Moses make his tea? Hebrews it.

CHAPTER 11: EASY RIDDLES

Everybody I know who is funny, it's in them. You can teach timing, or some people are able to tell a joke, though I don't like to tell jokes. But I think you have to be born with a sense of humor and a sense of timing.

Carol Burnett

1.   Which is the most curious letter?

A. Y?

2.   Why can't a man living in California be legally buried in New York (even if it's left as an instruction in his will)?

A. Because he's alive

3.   If a green man lives in a green house, a purple man lives in a purple house, a blue man lives in a

blue house, a yellow man lives in a yellow house, a black man lives in a black house. Who lives in a White house?

A. The President

4. Tool of thief, toy of queen. Always used to be unseen. Sign of joy, sign of sorrow. Giving all likeness borrowed.

A. A mask

5. Wednesday, Tom and Joe went to a restaurant and ate dinner. When they were done they paid for the food and left. But Tom and Joe didn't pay for the food. Who did?

A. Wednesday

6. What is the saddest fruit?

A. Blueberry

7. Who spends the day at the window, goes to the table for meals and hides at night?

A. Fly

8.   What language does a billboard speak?

A. Sign language

9.   What has four wheels and flies?

A. Garbage truck (flies)

10. What kind of key do you use on Thanksgiving?

A. A Turkey

11. If an electric train was going north at 100 miles/per hour which way would the smoke blow?

A. Electric trains don't blow smoke

12. A doctor and a bus driver are both in love with the same woman, an attractive girl named Sarah. The bus driver had to go on a long bus trip that would last a week. Before he left, he gave Sarah seven apples. Why?

A. An apple a day keeps the doctor away

13. What body part is pronounced as one letter but written with three, only two different letters are used?

A. Eye

14. What invention lets you look right through a wall?

A. A window

15. I'm where yesterday follows today and tomorrow is in the middle. What am I?

A. A dictionary

16. I have hands that wave you, though I never say goodbye. It's cool for you to be with me, especially when I say HI. What am I?

A. A fan

17. What do you call a rabbit with fleas?

A. Bugs bunny

18. What do you call a 100-year-old ant?

A. An antique

19. You go at red, but stop at green. What am I?

Watermelon! You eat the red part, and you stop eating at the green part.

20. Why is it so easy to weigh fish?

A. Because they have scales

21. How many of each species did Moses take on the ark with him?

A. None, Moses wasn't on the ark Noah was.

22. It can be cracked, It can be made, It can be told, it can be played. What is it?

A. Jokes

23. A kind of tree can you carry in your hand?

A. A palm

24. What can be opened but cannot be closed?

A. An egg

25. What kind of cup doesn't hold water?

A. Cupcake, Hiccup

26. Do you say, "Nine and five is thirteen," or "Nine and five are thirteen" ?

A. Neither. Nine and five are fourteen.

27. What has an eye but cannot see?

A. A needle

28. I am always in front and never behind. What am I?

A. The future

29. A boy fell off a 100 foot ladder. But he did not get hurt. Why not?

A. He was only on the first step

30. What has four eyes but can't see?

A. Mississippi

31. What can you catch but not throw?

A. A cold

32. What kind of table can you eat?

A. Vegetable

33. If April showers bring may flowers, what do may flowers bring?

A. Pilgrims

34. How can you drop a raw egg onto a concrete floor without cracking it?

A. It's highly likely the concrete floor will not crack

35. What is black and white and read all over?

A. Newspaper

36. If you eat me, my sender will eat you. What am I?

A. A fish hook

37. What's green, but not a leaf; copies others, but is not a monkey?

A. A parrot

38. We are brothers from the same mother, but we've never met.

A. Day and night

39. I'm as hard as a rock, but I melt immediately in hot water. What am I?

A. An ice cube

40. I use my ear to speak and my mouth to hear. What am I?

A. A phone

41. What's worth more after it's broken?

A. An egg

42. It's a shower, but without water.

A. A baby shower

43. You cannot come in or go out without me. What am I?

A. Door

44. You can see me in water, but I never get wet. What am I?

A. A reflection

45. Tuesday, Sam and Peter went to a restaurant to eat lunch. After eating lunch, they paid the bill. But Sam and Peter did not pay the bill, so who did?

Their friend, Tuesday

46. When it is alive we sing, when it is dead we clap our hands. What is it?

A. Birthday candles

47. Look at me. I can bring a smile to your face, a tear to your eye, or even a thought to your mind. But, I can't be seen. What am I?

A. Memories

48. A girl was ten on her last birthday, and will be twelve on her next birthday. How is this possible?

A. Today is her eleventh birthday

49. A woman is sitting in her hotel room when there is a knock at the door. She opened the door to see a man whom she had never seen before. He said "oh I'm sorry, I have made a mistake, I thought this was my room." He then went down the corridor and in the elevator. The woman went back into her room and phoned security. What made the woman so suspicious of the man?

A. You don't knock on your own hotel door and the man did.

50. What 4-letter word can be written forward, backward or upside down, and can still be read from left to right?

A. NOON

CHAPTER 12: HARDER RIDDLES

Whatever comes in my way, I take it with smile.

Kubra Sait

1. What has a Heart but no other organs?

A. A deck of cards

2. An old man wanted to leave all of his money to one of his three sons, but he didn't know which one he should give it to. He gave each of them a few coins and told them to buy something that would be able to fill their living room. The first man bought straw, but there was not enough to fill the room. The second bought some sticks, but they still did not fill the room. The third man bought two things that filled the room, so he obtained his father's fortune. What were the two things that the man bought?

A. The wise son bought a candle and a box of matches. After lighting the candle, the light filled the entire room.

3. Mr Brown was killed on Sunday afternoon. The wife said she was reading a book. The butler said He was taking a shower. The chef said he was making breakfast. The maid said she was folding clothes, and the gardener said he was planting tomatoes. Who did it?

A. The chef. Mr Brown was killed in the afternoon and yet the chef claimed he was making breakfast?

4. What is easy to get into, but hard to get out of?

A. Trouble

5. What is at the end of a rainbow?

A. The letter W

6. It is an insect, and the first part of its name is the name of another insect. What is it?

A. Beetle

7. What is harder to catch the faster you run?

A. Your breath

8. A snail is at the bottom of a 20 meters deep pit. Every day the snail climbs 5 meters upwards, but at night it slides 4 meters back downwards. How many days does it take before the snail reaches the top of the pit?

A. The snail reaches the top of the pit on the 16th day!

9. Forward I am heavy, but backward I am not. What am I?

A. Forward I am ton, backwards I am not

10. I have many teeth and sometimes they're fine, First I'm by your head, then I'm down your spine. What am I? What am I?

A. A comb

11. What English word has three consecutive double letters?

A. Bookkeeper

12. I never was, am always to be, No one ever saw me, nor ever will And yet I am the confidence of all To live and breathe on this terrestrial ball. What is it?

A. Tomorrow

13. A man wants to enter an exclusive club, but he doesn't know the password. Another man walks to the door and the doorman says 12, the man says 6, and is let in. Another man walks up and the doorman says 6, the man says 3, and is let in. Thinking he had heard enough, he walks up to the door and the doorman says 10, he says 5, and he isn't let in. What should he have said?

A. Three. He should have said how many letters were in the number he said.

14. There are two planes. One is going from New York to London at a speed of 600 MPH. The other is travelling from London to New York at a speed of 500 MPH. When the planes meet which one will be closer to London?

A. They will be the same distance away when they meet.

15. If you go to the movies and you're paying, is it cheaper to take one friend to the movies twice, or two friends to the movies at the same time?

A. It's cheaper to take two friends at the same time. In this case, you would only be buying three tickets, whereas if you take the same friend twice you are buying four tickets.

16. People buy me to eat, but never eat me. What am I?

A. Plates and cuttlery

17. A murderer is condemned to death. He has to choose between three rooms. The first is full of raging fires, the second is full of assassins with loaded guns, and the third is full of lions that haven't eaten in 3 years. Which room is safest for him?

A. The third room. Lions that haven't eaten in three years are dead.

18. If you were standing directly on the south pole facing north, which direction would you travel if you took one step backward?

A. North

19. You are playing a game of dodge ball with two other people, John and Tom. You're standing in a triangle and you all take turns throwing at one of the others of your choosing until there is only one person remaining. You have a 30 percent chance of hitting someone you aim at, John has a 50 percent chance, and Tom a 100 percent change (he never misses). If you hit somebody they are out and no longer get a turn. If the order of

throwing is you, John, then Tom; what should you do to have the best chance of winning?

A. Miss the first time on purpose. If you try to hit John and do. Then Tom goes next and he will hit you and you will lose for sure. If you aim at Tom and hit him then John will go for you. If you miss on your first turn John will go for Tom for sure because he is a stronger player. If he hits him then it's just you and John, but you are going first. If he misses him then Tom will hit John and it will be just you and Tom, but again in this case you are going first.

20. I have one, you have one. If you remove the first letter, a bit remains. If you remove the second, bit still remains. After much trying, you might be able to remove the third one also, but it remains. It dies hard!

A. Habit! Remove h and "a bit" remains; remove a and "bit" remains; remove b and "it" remains.

21. A man is trapped in a room. The room has only two possible exits: two doors. Through the first door there is a room constructed from magnifying glass. The blazing hot sun instantly fries anything or anyone that enters. Through the second door there is a fire-breathing dragon. How does the man escape?

A. He waits until night time and then goes through the first door.

22. A king has no sons, no daughters, and no queen. For this reason he must decide who will take the throne after he dies. To do this he decides that he will give all of the children of the kingdom a single seed. Whichever child has the largest, most beautiful plant will earn the throne; this being a metaphor for the kingdom. At the end of the contest all of the children came to the palace with their enormous and beautiful plants in hand. After he looks at all of the children's pots, he finally decides that the little girl with an empty pot will be the next Queen. Why did he choose this little girl over all of the other children with their beautiful plants?

A. The king gave them all fake seeds and the little girl was the only honest child who didn't switch seeds.

23. I am a ship that can be made to ride the greatest waves. I am not built by tool, but built by hearts and minds. What am I?

A. Friendship

24. I have two arms, but fingers none. I have two feet, but cannot run. I carry well, but I have found I

carry best with my feet off the ground. What am I?

A. Wheelbarrow

25. I can be long, or I can be short. I can be grown, and I can be bought. I can be painted, or left bare. I can be round, or square. What am I?

A. Fingernails

26. I am a fruit. If you take away the first letter of my name I become a crime. Take away the first two letters of my name I become an animal. Take away the first and last letter of my name and I become a form of music. What am I?

A. Grape Rape Ape Rap

27. You are in a room with 3 monkeys. One monkey has a banana, one has a stick, and one has nothing. Who is the smartest primate?

A. You

28. What can travel around the world while staying in a corner?

A. A stamp

29. What gets broken without being held?

A. A promise

30. What has cities, but no houses; forests, but no trees; and water, but no fish?

A. A map

31. two in a corner, 1 in a room, 0 in a house, but 1 in a shelter. What am I?

A. The letter r

32. I can fly but have no wings. I can cry but I have no eyes. Wherever I go, darkness follows me. What am I?

A. Clouds

33. The more you take, the more you leave behind. What am I?

A. Footsteps

34. I'm tall when I'm young, I'm short when I'm old. What am I?

A. Candle / Pencil

35. I'm excellent to taste, but horrible to smell. What am I?

A. A tongue

36. I have lots of money, but I need someone else to carry me around to spend it.

A. A wallet/purse.

37. I am a number. When you add the letter G to me, I go away. What number am I?

A. One (add G and it becomes 'gone')

38. I am made of water, but I'm not wet. What am I?

A. A cloud

39. I am black in colour, yet I'm colourless. What am I?

A. A shadow

40. I'm a single digit number having no value. Which number am I?

Answer: Number 0 (zero)

41. What grows only upwards and can never come down?

A. Our height

42. What has teeth, but cannot chew?

A. A comb

43. I have hands, but cannot hold a thing.

A. A clock

44. I can carry lots of food, but cannot eat anything.

A. A refrigerator

45. It can see, but it isn't an eye. What is it?

A. A keyhole

46. What is it that you can't hold for more than a few seconds?

A. Your breath

47. You can eat me at night, but never in the morning. What am I?

A. Dinner

48. I am hard like stone, but I grow on your body. What am I?

A. A tooth

49. You cannot come in or go out without me. What am I?

A. Door

CHAPTER 13: FOOD RIDDLES

I love those who can smile in trouble, who can gather strength from distress, and grow brave by reflection. 'Tis the business of little minds to shrink, but they whose heart is firm, and whose conscience approves their conduct, will pursue their principles unto death.

Leonardo da Vinci

1. What has ears but cannot hear?

Answer: Corn

2. What has eyes but cannot see?

Answer: A potato

3. What kind of room has no windows or doors?

Answer: Mushroom

4. What stinks when living and smells good when dead?

Answer: Bacon

5. What has a heart that does not beat yet it lives?

Answer: An artichoke

6. It can poison water in a way no detect poison can tell you. Damned it is in water, highly priced when dry.

Answer: Salt

7. Hundreds of black smiths, in a dungeon with no doors or windows, when we leave, each of us builds his own dungeon.

Answer: Watermelon

8. I come out of the earth, I am sold in the market. He who buys me cuts off my tail, takes off my suit of silk, and weeps beside me when I am dead.

Answer: Onion

9. A red cap on my head, a stone in my throat, if you tell me the answer, I'll give you a Groat. What am I?

Answer: Peach

10. Alive without breath, As cold as death; Never thirsty, ever drinking, All in mail never clinking.

Answer: Fish

11. Crushed beneath trampling feet, kept in darkness and cold. I am useless if I have suffered not; but having suffered, my temper is sweet and strong to all those who partake. What am I, at start?

Answer: Grapes

12. In marble halls as white as milk, lined with skin as soft as silk. Within a fountain crystal clear, a golden apple doth appear. No doors there are to this stronghold, Yet thieves break in and steal the gold.

Answer: Egg

13. Remove the outside, cook the inside, eat the outside, throw away the inside.

Answer: Corn

14. I am seeking for a dark gold, highly priced by young and old, since I couldn´t find it in any vault. I will take a bite tasting if it is right.

Answer: Chocolate

15. Squeeze it and it cries tears as red as it's flesh. It's heart is made of stone.

Answer: Cherry

16. What has no beginning, end, or middle?

Answer: A doughnut

17. Why did the tomato blush?

A. Because it saw the salad dressing.

18. Why don't eggs tell jokes?

A. They would crack each other up.

19. Why is it a bad idea to tell secrets on a farm?

A. Because the potatoes have eyes and the corn has ears.

20. What kind of nut seems to have a cold?

Answer: Cashews.

21. Why do watermelons have fancy weddings?

Answer: Because they cantaloupe.

22. What happens to grapes when you step on them?

Answer: They wine.

23. What is the difference between a unicorn and a carrot?

Answer: One is a funny beast and the other is a bunny feast.

24. Why did the baker stop making doughnuts?

Answer: Because he was tired of the hole business.

25. What do you get when you cross a chicken and a caterpillar?

Answer: Enough drumsticks for everyone.

26. Why did the cookie go to the doctor?

Answer: He was feeling crumby.

27. What is a pelican's favorite dish?

Answer: Anything that fits the bill.

28. How do you make an elephant sandwich?

Answer: First you take a giant loaf of bread. . . .

29. Why did the little boy stare at the can of orange juice?

Answer: Because it said, "Concentrate."

30. What's the worst thing about being an octopus?

Answer: Washing up before dinner.

31. What did one knife say to the other?

Answer: "Be sharp!"

32. How do you fix a pizza?

Answer: With tomato paste.

33. Why was the cook arrested?

Answer: Because he beat the eggs and whipped the cream.

34. What kind of pizza did the cannibal order?

Answer: One with everyone on it.

35. Why don't they serve chocolate in jail?

Answer: Because it makes you break out.

36. What did the cake say to the fork?

Answer: "You want a piece of me?"

37. Why did the little boy put candy under his pillow?

Answer: He wanted sweet dreams.

38. What does bread do after it's baked?

Answer: It loafs around.

39. Old McDonald owns me. What am I?

Answer: A Farm

40. 72. I spit a lot. You can get wool from me. What
am I?

Answer: A Llama

41. What is Santa Claus' favorite sandwich?

A. Peanut Butter and Jolly!

42. I go to McDonalds, I order food, my food cost less
than $20, I hand them $20, I got my food, drink,
dessert, and receipt. What did I forget?

A. I forgot my change!

43. What do you call a nervous zucchini?

A. An Edgy Veggie.

44. Two mother's and two daughters went out to eat. They each had one burger, yet only three burgers were eaten. How is this possible?

A. There was a grandmother, mother, and a daughter.

45. Where do pretzels go on vacation?

A. Pretzelvania

46. What did the grouchy baker make?

A. Crab cakes

47. *Clean, but not water,*

White, but not snow,

Sweet, but not ice-cream,

What is it?

A. Sugar

48. *Boil meat and veggies and I taste just right*

If you're not feeling well I can ease your appetite

A. Soup

CHAPTER 14: FUNNY RIDDLES

I'm writing a book. I've got the page numbers done.

Steven Wright

1. Brothers and sisters have I none but that man's father is my father's son.

Answer: Looking at yourself in a mirror

2. A box without hinges, key, or lid yet golden treasure inside is hid. What is it?

Answer: Egg

3. What letter comes next: O T T F F S S ?

Answer: e-eight

4. All about the house, with his lady he dances. Yet he always works, and never romances.

Answer: Broom

5. My life can be measured in hours, I serve by being devoured. Thin, I am quick. Fat, I am slow. Wind is my foe.

Answer: Candle

6. I am a precious little thing, dancing and eating all the time. Watch me from a distance, so you can feel my warm and gentle love. But don't come to close or my next meal you could be!

Answer: Fire

7. George walked for thirty minutes in the pouring rain without getting a single hair on his head wet. He didn't have a hat or an umbrella and his coat had no hood.

How did he do that?

Answer: He is bald

8. What stays where it is when it goes off?

Answer: An alarm clock.

9. What needs an answer but doesn't ask a question?

Answer: A telephone.

10. If you took two apples from three apples how many apples would you have?

Answer: Two apples – the two that you took.

11. What fur do we get from a Tiger?

Answer: As fur away as possible!

12. Why did the woman wear a helmet at the dinner table?

Answer: Because of her crash diet

13. Why was the belt arrested?

Answer: For holding up the pants

14. What do you call a funny book about eggs?

Answer: Yolk book

15. What is the best cure for dandruff?

Answer: Baldness

16. What do you call a man who does not have all his fingers on one hand?

Answer: Normal – You have fingers on both hands!

17. What does an invisible man drink at snack time?

Answer: Evaporated milk

18. Why can't you play basketball with pigs?

Answer: Because they hog the ball

19. Which football player wears the biggest helmet?

Answer: The one with the biggest head

20. What did the outlaw get when he stole a calendar?

Answer: Twelve months

21. In which month do monkeys play baseball?

Answer: Ape-ril

22. What is the longest word in the dictionary?

Answer: Smiles, because there is a mile between each "s"

23. What goes through towns and over hills but never moves?

Answer: A road

24. What is something you will never see again?

Answer: Yesterday

25. Jack rode into town on Friday and rode out two days later on Friday. How can that be possible?

Answer: Friday is his horse's name

26. A lawyer, a plumber, and a hat maker were walking down the street. Who had the biggest hat?

Answer: The one with the biggest head

27. Who is the fastest runner in the whole world?

Answer: Adam. Because he was the first in the human race

28. I have keys but no doors, I have space but no rooms, I allow you to enter but you are never able to leave. What am I?

Answer: A keyboard

29. I have wings, I am able to fly, I'm not a bird yet I soar high in the sky. What am I?

Answer: An airplane

30. Why is Cinderella a bad football player?

A. Because she has a pumpkin as a coach!

31. What do you get when you mix a German Shepard and a giraffe?

A. A watch dog for the fifteenth floor!

32. What colour is a burp?

A. BURPle!

33. What kind of bus crossed the ocean?

A. Christopher ColumBUS!

34. Whoever makes it, tells it not. Whoever takes it, knows it not. Whoever knows it, wants it not. What is it?

A. Counterfeit money.

35. What did the creek say to the brook?

A. "Stop babbling!"

36. What has two heads, one tail and six legs?

A. A man on a horse.

37. Which wolf got lost in the woods?

A. The WHEREwolf.

38. What is black and white, black and white, black and white, black and white, black and white and green?

A. Two skunks fighting over a pickle.

39. If you are running in a race and you just passed the guy in second place what place are you in?

A. You are in second place!

40. What type of soap did the composer use?

A. Anti-BACH-terial.

41. How do you make varnish disappear?

A. Take away the R!

42. What has two back bones and 1000 ribs?

A. A railroad.

43. What animal is NOT allowed to play in games or contests?

A. Cheetahs (cheaters)

44. What did the tornado ask the car?

A. "Wanna go for a spin?"

45. What did the big hand on the clock say to the little hand?

A. "Hour you today?"

46. Why couldn't the skeleton laugh?

A. Because he lost his funny bone

47. How do you communicate with a fish?

A. Drop it a line.

48. What is a cow's favorite ice cream?

A. MOOnila!

49. If I did this equation, 23x45+27x99= What answer would I get?

A. A very big number!

50. Who was the first deer in space?

A. Buck Rogers.

51. What do you call an overweight E.T.?

A. Extra Cholesterol!

52. What do you call a rabbit with the sniffles?

A. A runny bunny.

53. What's a frog's favorite year?

A. Leap year!

54. What does a French cow say?

A. "Moo Lala!"

CHAPTER 15: CONCLUSION

Wow! You made it through all 700 of the hilarious jokes and mind twisting riddles in this book.... How did they go? Did you have fun? These jokes have all been hand picked in order to make you laugh like there's no tomorrow! We hope you enjoyed going through them and they created some great memories between you, your friends and your family.

Once again, we would like to thank you for reading our book *The Jumbo Jokes and Riddles Book part 2* and we can't wait to hear what you thought about it. If you enjoyed listening to this book, please don't forget to leave a review and let us know exactly how much you loved it. Reviews mean the world to us and help us continue to create books just like this one for years to come.

Thank you!

DL Digital Entertainment

Made in the USA
Coppell, TX
17 March 2020

17090053R00090